Quick Tips from a Pro Photographer

Book 1

Starting Out

By Julia K Harwood

Contents

Table of Contents

Introduction

I have learned a lot of tips on my photographic journey, from shooting images, reading articles and doing courses, so I wanted to bring them together here so that you can learn much easier and quicker than I did.

I will be doing a series of mini e-books so that you can have the tips handy and you can work on one section at a time, once you feel confident with that then you move onto the next one. If you have a special event coming up, then you can jump to the quick tips for that subject, be it a wedding, a graduation or the birth of a baby.

I have been a photographer for over 20 years but I want you to have this information at your fingers so that photography is fun and you are not having to spend a lot of time, money and effort to learn these 'tricks of the trade'.

So let's get started!

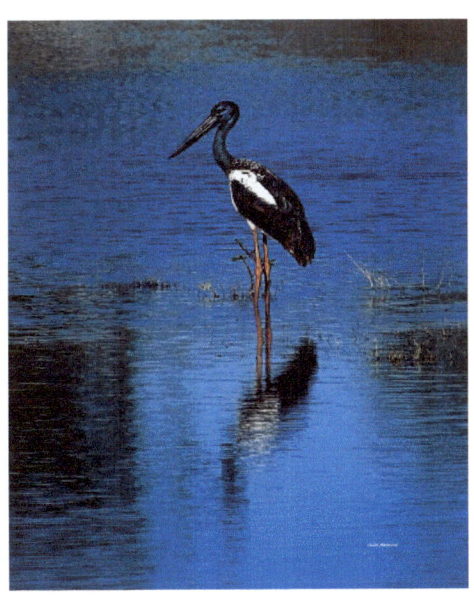

2.Be prepared

Like a good boy scout or girl guide the motto of being prepared is essential, in photography and in today's mobile world it is easier than ever.

The first part of being prepared is to always have your camera with you. This used to take an effort to pack your camera with you, now with phones with cameras we usually have a camera with us anyway, so being prepared is more about remembering that we have this great tool and remembering to pull it out and use it.

The latest phones not only give you photos, but videos, panorama and time lapse, so it's time to get them out and have some fun.

3.Learn how to use your camera.

This sounds really obvious, but you would be surprised at how many people don't.

Whether it's your phone, point and shoot, bridge or full DSLR it really pays to go through the manual so you know how it works.

I hear your howls of, "it's too much technical jibber jabber."

Most people could read the manual 10 times and still not understand it. So this next tip will show you how to do it.

4. Work through the manual one chapter or section at a time.

Have your camera beside you and look at the settings the manual is talking about and then spend a day or a week just using that setting so that you become familiar with it.

As you run into difficulties you go back to the manual and read that section again, because you are doing rather than just reading it will begin to make sense.

Once you feel you understand that bit move onto the next chapter. It may take a while to get through it, but you are using it in the meantime and learning by doing, this is much more fun than just trying to read and understand it.

5.Have fun.

Have a day a week where you don't worry about settings, instead you just put it on auto or the scene modes and shoot away at anything, not worrying about technicalities, just enjoying the thrill of spontaneity.

When you look back at the images if there are some you really love then study them and try to work out why they work. Which takes us to the next tip.

6.Learn from the meta data.

Oh no, there's that technical jibber jabber again.

What is Meta Data?

Meta data is just the information about the shot.

It tells us what shutter speed, what focal length, what aperture and what ISO we used.

In today's digital age it is automatically embedded in the image and you can usual find it by right clicking on an image and going to properties.

It also tells you the time you took it, whether or not the flash fired and some modern cameras even have the GPS coordinates of where it was taken.

This is a great way to start learning about settings and what works and what doesn't.

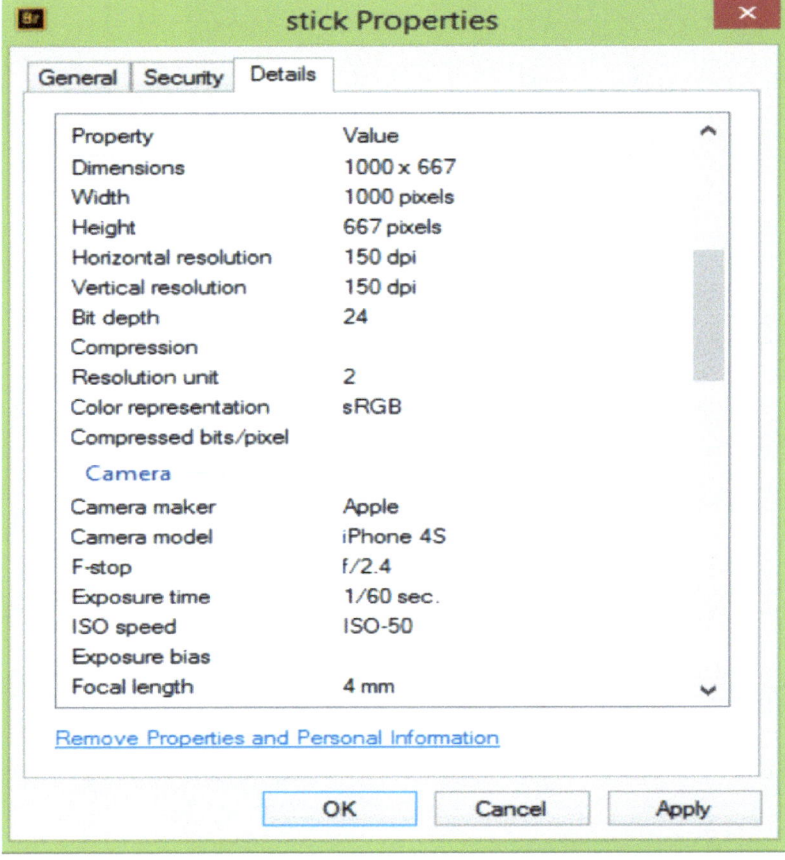

7.Seeing.

How often have you heard the saying, "you've got a good eye"

This is the ability to see what is in an image and present it in such a way as is appealing to the general public.

Seeing can be learned, so here are two ways to get started.

First when you see something you want to photograph ask yourself, "what is the story I want to share with the viewer?"

Then look at the elements in the scene and ask, "does this add to the story?"

If it does leave it in, if it doesn't move it if possible, if not move yourself to find a position where you can angle it out of shot, you can also use a small depth of field to do this as well.

More on that later.

The second part of 'seeing' is looking at the light.

- What direction is it coming from?

- Are the shadows it creates hard or soft?

- What effect is it having on the scene?

- Where are the shadows, do they obscure the main subject?

- Is the light dappled?

Photography is painting with light, so we need to start being aware of it. Practice seeing light whenever you are outside walking, then it will become second nature when you are taking photographs.

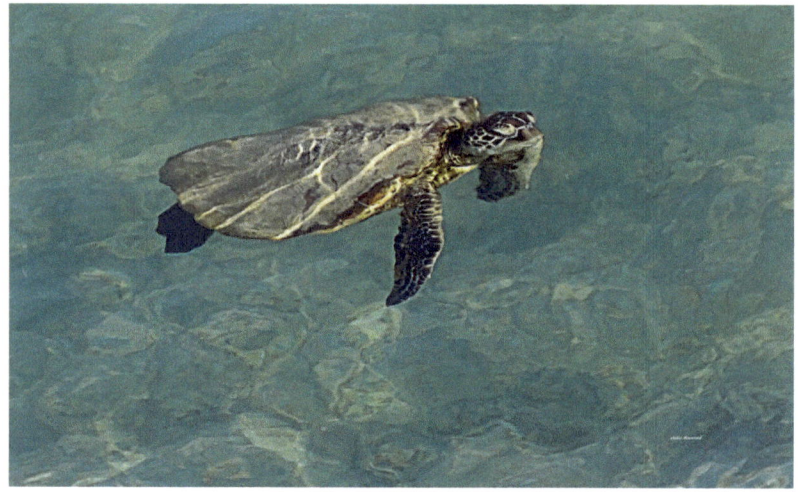

8.Set yourself challenges.

Often we think what am I going to shoot, there is nothing exciting around here.

So give yourself a challenge,

- Photograph only blue today, or any other color.

- Capture the alphabet in shapes.

- Move closer.
(*This one especially is really important. When you think you are close enough take a shot, then move closer again and take another one.*)

- Photograph one object only, take photos that have one object in them and nothing else.

- Take pictures of people.

I'm sure, if you try, you can think of many more. Whenever you think of an idea jot it down or add it to your phone notes and next time you are stuck you have a list ready to go.

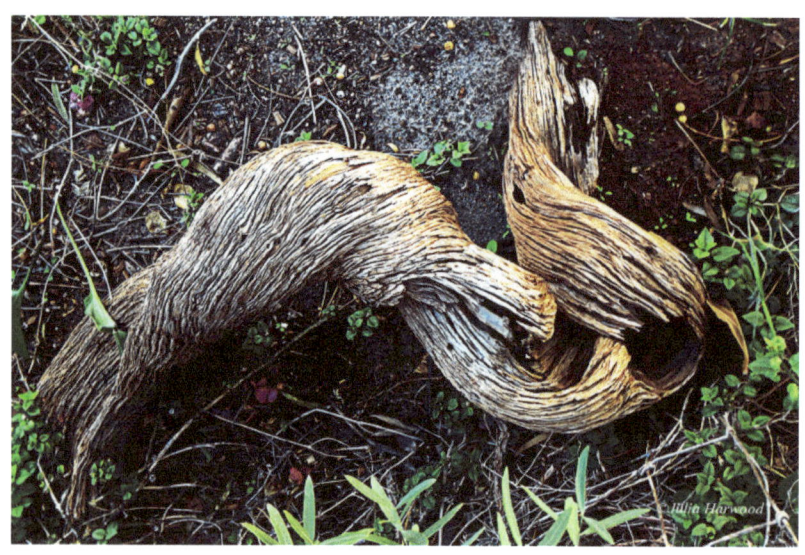

9. Scene modes

These are fantastic tools to get you started in photography.

Most cameras have these.

You may see little icons on your dial like a mountain for landscape, someone running for sports, a flower for close ups and a sun for sunset. Other cameras will just have S or SP, when you move the dial here you can choose from a list of topics. Newer cameras even have special scene modes for dogs and cats and babies, toy camera, selective color and more.

So dial up the scene you are shooting and happily shoot away.

10.Stance

This is the final tip for this e-book, it is the way we stand when taking a shot.

Yes it does make a difference, while you can stand on your head and take a photo or lay flat out on the ground, hang from the monkey bars or shoot while jumping out of a plane, most of the time we will be upright and on two feet.

Place one foot a bit behind the other, this gives us back to front stability.

Keep your elbows by your side, this enables your body to act as a monopod or a vertical support.

Hold the camera grip with one hand and the lens with the other hand.

Use the viewfinder if possible, this allows our face to support the camera, when you hold it out in front looking at the screen we have more chance of getting a shaky image

Finally as you press the shutter hold your breath and roll your finger off the shutter instead of lifting it off. You won't need to do this all the time, but when you are getting below 1/60 sec shutter speed it may just help you get that great shot without it being blurred.

Happy shooting.

I would love to see your images, so go to my website at http://www.juliaharwood.com/getting-started and you can add your photos or comments there, you can also sign up to my newsletter and get some freebies as well.

If you found this helpful then have a look at the rest of the books in the series. (link here)

I also have a Youtube channel where I do tutorial videos on post processing with Photoshop. Even though I use photoshop, there are tips that can help you no matter what software you use.

Go here to see it: https://www.youtube.com/channel/UCpGMVjhAPmXk_hgVOBHS1Gw

Cheat Sheet

~ Starting out ~

1. Be prepared, have you got a camera with you?
2. Learn how to use it.
3. Have fun!
4. Metadata, what is it telling you?
5. Seeing, where is the light, where are the shadows?
6. Set yourself challenges, get closer, one colour, one subject, letters.
7. Use scene modes.
8. Watch how you are standing, hold your breath as you push the shutter.

I have deliberately created the cheat sheet with a smaller font so that you can print it out and laminate it, at the end of the series you will have a set you can carry with you.
Punch a hole in the corner and put them on a keyring. Below is an example.

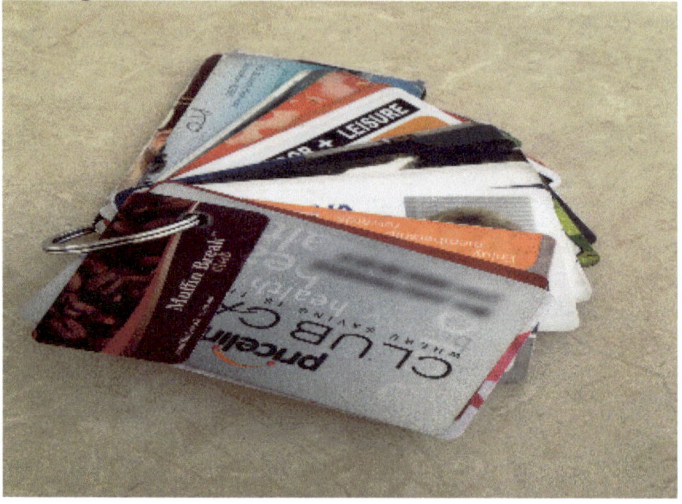

Special Thanks

I would like to make a special mention of a few people who without their support this series would not be possible. Firstly to my Proof Reader, Cathy Longley, no matter how sick you were you still managed to get these done, thank you so much. The to all my supporters on Pozible but most especially Angela Chan, as without her financial backing this project would not have been possible and finally to my wonderful husband Colin, who put up with me spending so many hours on the computer. I hope these help you on your photographic journey.

You can also follow me on my website at Photography by Julia K Harwood
http://www.juliaharwood.com/

For all your gift needs
http://www.redbubble.com/people/juliakharwood/portfolio

To follow me on G+
http://plus.google.com/+JuliaHarwood

To follow on FB
http://m.facebook.com/Photography.by.Julia.K.Harwood

To view a gallery of my images
http://photographybyjuliakharwood.shootproof.com/juliaharwood

www.ingramcontent.com/pod-product-compliance
Lightning Source LLC
Chambersburg PA
CBHW041618180526
45159CB00002BC/917